All of Me, Stay with Me & More Hot Singles

T0066245

ISBN 978-1-4950-1058-3

HAL•LEONARD®
CORPORATION
7777 W. BLUEMOUND RD. P.O. BOX 13819 MILWAUKEE, WI 53213

Visit Hal Leonard Online at
www.halleonard.com

RHYTHM TAB LEGEND

Rhythm Tab is a form of notation that adds rhythmic values to the traditional tab staff.

TABLATURE graphically represents the guitar fingerboard. Each horizontal line represents a string, and each number represents a fret. Rhythmic values are shown using ovals, stems, and dots.

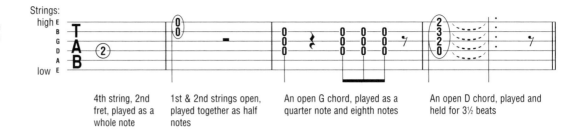

4th string, 2nd fret, played as a whole note

1st & 2nd strings open, played together as half notes

An open G chord, played as a quarter note and eighth notes

An open D chord, played and held for 3½ beats

Definitions for Special Guitar Notation

HALF-STEP BEND: Strike the note and bend up 1/2 step.

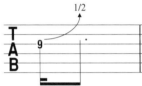

WHOLE-STEP BEND: Strike the note and bend up one step.

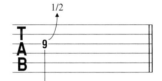

GRACE NOTE BEND: Strike the note and immediately bend up as indicated.

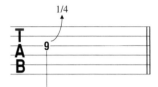

SLIGHT (MICROTONE) BEND: Strike the note and bend up 1/4 step.

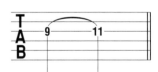

BEND AND RELEASE: Strike the note and bend up as indicated, then release back to the original note. Only the first note is struck.

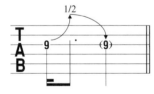

PRE-BEND: Bend the note as indicated, then strike it.

PRE-BEND AND RELEASE: Bend the note as indicated. Strike it and release the bend back to the original note.

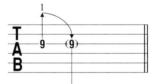

UNISON BEND: Strike the two notes simultaneously and bend the lower note up to the pitch of the higher.

HOLD BEND: While sustaining bent note, strike note on different string.

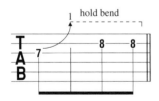

VIBRATO: The string is vibrated by rapidly bending and releasing the note with the fretting hand.

WIDE VIBRATO: The pitch is varied to a greater degree by vibrating with the fretting hand.

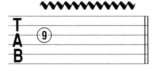

HAMMER-ON: Strike the first (lower) note with one finger, then sound the higher note (on the same string) with another finger by fretting it without picking.

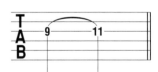

PULL-OFF: Place both fingers on the notes to be sounded. Strike the first note and without picking, pull the finger off to sound the second (lower) note.

HAMMER FROM NOWHERE: Sound note(s) by hammering with fret hand finger only.

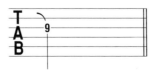

GRACE NOTE SLUR: Strike the note and immediately hammer-on (or pull-off) as indicated.

GRACE NOTE SLUR (CLUSTER): Strike the notes and immediately hammer-on (or pull-off) as indicated.

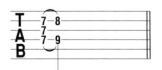

Contents

All of Me

Words and Music by John Stephens and Toby Gad

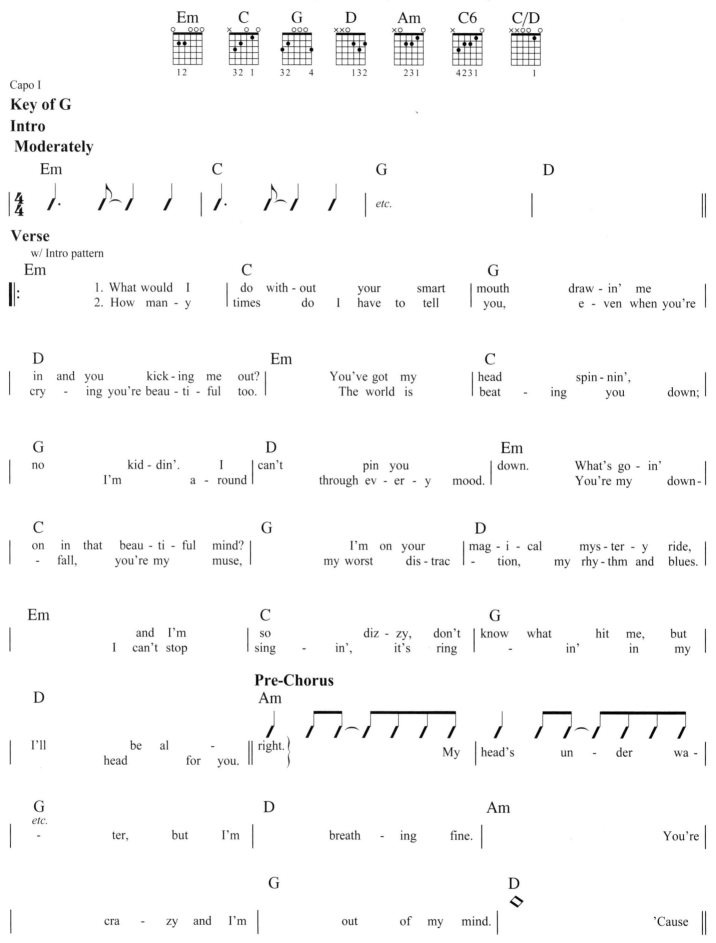

⸭ Chorus

3rd time, let chords ring (next 8 meas.)

G   Em

| all   of me | loves | all   of you. | Love your |

C6   C/D   D

| curves and all your edg - es,   all your | per - fect im - per - fec - tions. Give your |

3rd time, resume strumming pattern

G   Em

| all   to me,   I'll give my | all   to you. | You're my |

C6   C/D   D

| end and my be - gin - ning.   E - ven | when I lose, I'm win - ning 'cause I give you all |

Em   C   G   D

| | of me. | And you give me all |

3rd time, To Coda ⊕

Em   C   G   1. D   2. D

| | of you, | oh. | :|| Give me all of you. ||

Bridge

Am   G   D

| | Cards   on   the   ta - ble, we're both | show - ing   hearts. |

D.S. al Coda

Am   G   D

| | Risk - ing   it   all, | though it's hard. | 'Cause ||

⊕ Coda

G   D   Em   C   G

| | I give you all | | of me. | |

D   Em   C   G   D

| | And you give me all | | of you, | oh. | ||

Let Her Go

Words and Music by Michael David Rosenberg

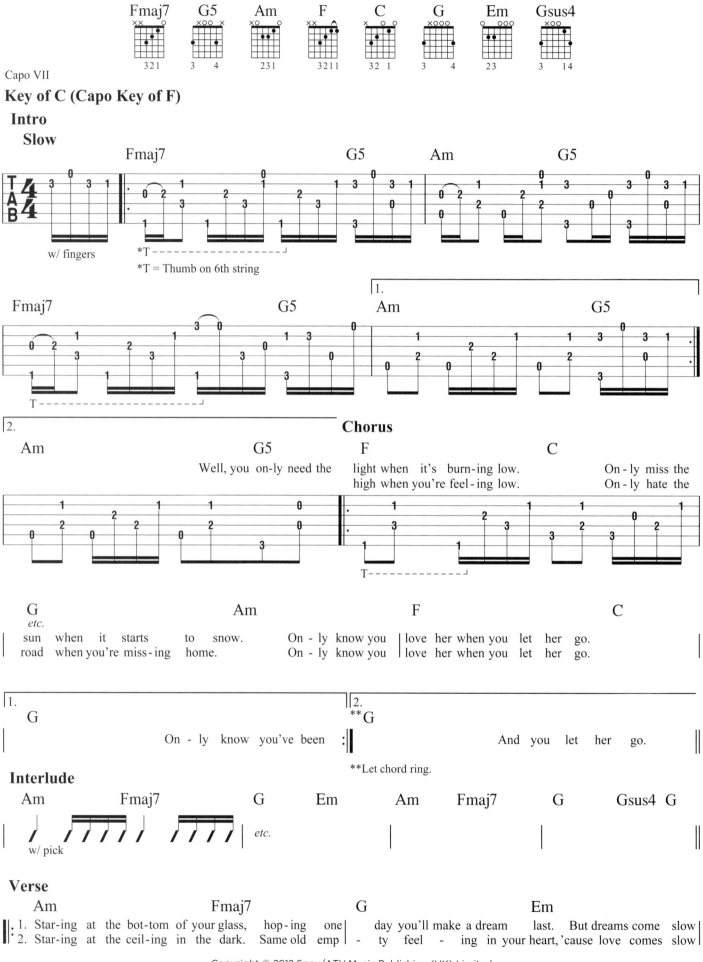

Capo VII

Key of C (Capo Key of F)

Intro

Slow

w/ fingers

*T = Thumb on 6th string

Chorus

Well, you on-ly need the light when it's burn-ing low. On-ly miss the
high when you're feel-ing low. On-ly hate the

sun when it starts to snow. On-ly know you love her when you let her go.
road when you're miss-ing home. On-ly know you love her when you let her go.

On - ly know you've been

And you let her go.

**Let chord ring.

Interlude

w/ pick

etc.

Verse

1. Star-ing at the bot-tom of your glass, hop-ing one day you'll make a dream last. But dreams come slow
2. Star-ing at the ceil-ing in the dark. Same old emp-ty feel-ing in your heart, 'cause love comes slow

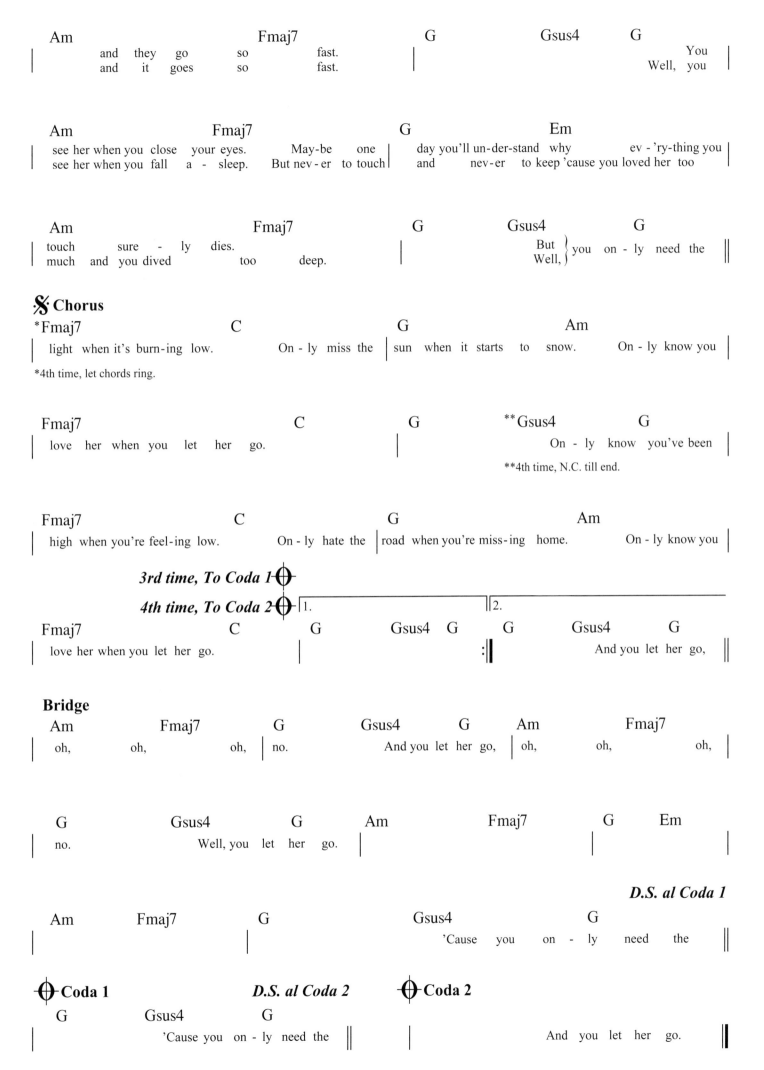

Riptide

Words and Music by Vance Joy

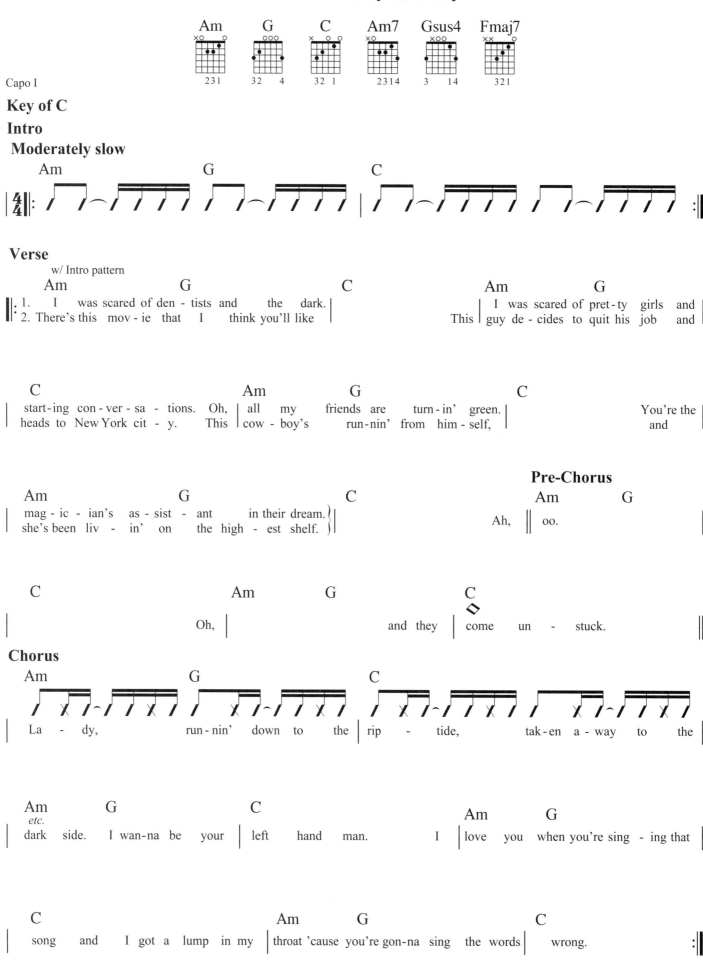

Capo I

Key of C

Intro

Moderately slow

Verse
w/ Intro pattern

1. I was scared of den - tists and   the dark.   I was scared of pret - ty girls and
2. There's this mov - ie that I   think you'll like   This | guy de - cides to quit his job and

start - ing con - ver - sa - tions. Oh, | all my friends are turn - in' green.   You're the
heads to New York cit - y.   This | cow - boy's   run - nin' from him - self,   and

mag - ic - ian's as - sist - ant   in their dream. |
she's been liv - in' on   the high - est shelf. |

Pre-Chorus

Ah, | oo.

Oh, | and they | come un - stuck.

Chorus

La - dy,   run - nin' down to the | rip - tide,   tak - en a - way to the

etc.
dark side. I wan - na be your | left hand man.   I | love you when you're sing - ing that

song and I got a lump in my | throat 'cause you're gon - na sing the words | wrong.

Interlude

N.C.(C)

Bridge

Am7		Gsus4	G		C	

I just wan - na, I just wan-na know | if you're gon - na, if you're gon-na stay.

Fmaj7		Am7			Gsus4	G

I just got - ta, I just got-ta know; |

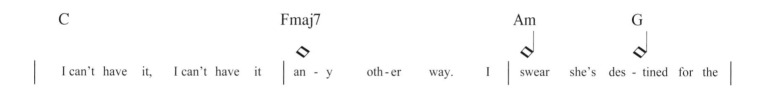

C		Fmaj7		Am	G	

I can't have it, I can't have it | an - y oth-er way. I | swear she's des - tined for the |

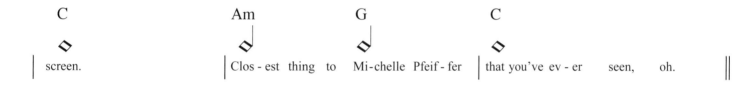

C		Am	G		C	

screen. | Clos - est thing to Mi-chelle Pfeif-fer | that you've ev - er seen, oh. ‖

Chorus

w/ Chorus pattern

Am	G		C		Am	G

‖: La - dy, run-nin' down to the | rip - tide, tak-en a-way to the | dark side. I wan-na be your

C		Am	G		C	

left hand man. I | love you when you're sing - ing that | song and I got a lump in my

			1., 2.		3.	
Am	G		C		C	

throat 'cause you're gon na sing the words | wrong. :‖ wrong, yeah. I got a lump in my

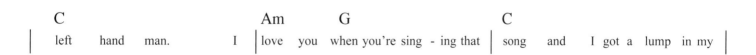

Am		G			C	

grad. slower

throat 'cause you're gon - na sing the words | wrong. ‖

Stay with Me

Words and Music by Sam Smith, James Napier and William Edward Phillips

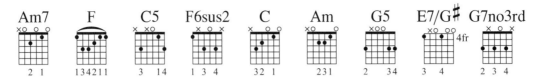

Key of C

Intro

Moderately slow

Am7   F   C5   Am7   F   C5

4/4 | *etc.* | | ||

Verse

Am7   F   C5

1. Guess it's true, I'm not good at a one-night | stand.
2. Why am I so e-mo-tion - | al?

Am7   F   C5

But I still need love 'cause I'm just a | man.
No, it's not a good look. Gain some self - con - | trol.

Am7   F   C5

These nights nev - er seem to go to | plan.
And deep down I know this nev - er | works.

Am7   *F6sus2   C

I don't want you to leave, will you hold my | hand? }
But you can lay with me so it does - n't | hurt. }   Oh, won't you ||

*2nd time, substitute G7no3rd.

Chorus

Am   F   C   Am   F   C

| stay with me? | 'Cause you're | all I need. |

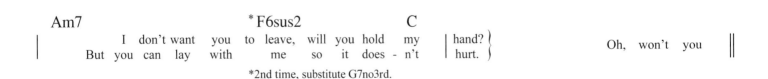

G5	Am	F	C		E7/G#
This ain't	love, it's clear to see.				But, dar - ling,

Am	F	C		**1.**	**2.**
stay	with me.				Oh,

Bridge

Am	F	C		Am7	F	C
		oh.				

1.	**2.**	**Outro-Chorus**		
Oh,	Oh, won't you	Am	F	C
		stay with me?		

Am	F	C		G5
'Cause you're	all I need.			This ain't

Am	F	C		E7/G#	**1.** Am	F6sus2	C
love, it's clear to see.				But, dar - ling,	stay	with	me.

2. Am	F	C	
Oh, won't you	stay with me.		

Take Me to Church

Words and Music by Andrew Hozier-Byrne

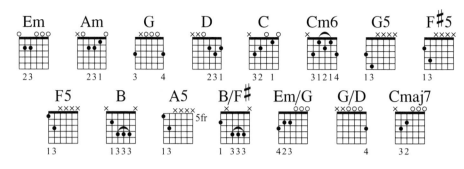

Key of Em

Verse

Slow (♪♪ = ♪♪)

let chords ring

Em	Am	Em	Am	G	Am
3/4 1. My lov-er's got hu-mour.		She's the gig-gle at a fun-'ral.		Knows ev-'ry-bod-y's dis-ap-prov-al.	

Em	Am	Em	Am
I should've wor-shipped her soon-er.		‖: 2. If the heav-ens e-ver did speak,	
		If I'm a pa-gan of the good times,	

Em	Am	G	Am
she's the last true mouth-piece.		Ev-'ry Sun-day's get-ting more bleak.	
my lov-er's the sun-light.		To keep the god-dess on my side,	

Em	Am	D	C
A fresh poi-son each week.		4/4 "We were born sick," you heard them say it.	3/4
she de-mands a sac-ri-fice.		Drain the whole sea, get some-thin' shin-y.	

Em	Am	Em	Am
3/4 My church of-fers no ab-so-lutes.		She tells me, "Wor-ship in the bed-room."	
Some-thin' meat-y for the main course.		That's a fine look-in' high horse.	

G	Am	Em	Am
The on-ly heav-en I'll be sent to		is when I'm a-lone with you.	4/4
What you got in the sta-ble?		We've a lot of starv-in' faith-ful.	

2nd time, skip To Chorus

D	C		
4/4 I was born sick, but I love it.		Com-mand me to be well. A,	3/4
That looks tast-y, that looks plen-ty.		This is hun-gry work. Take me to church.	

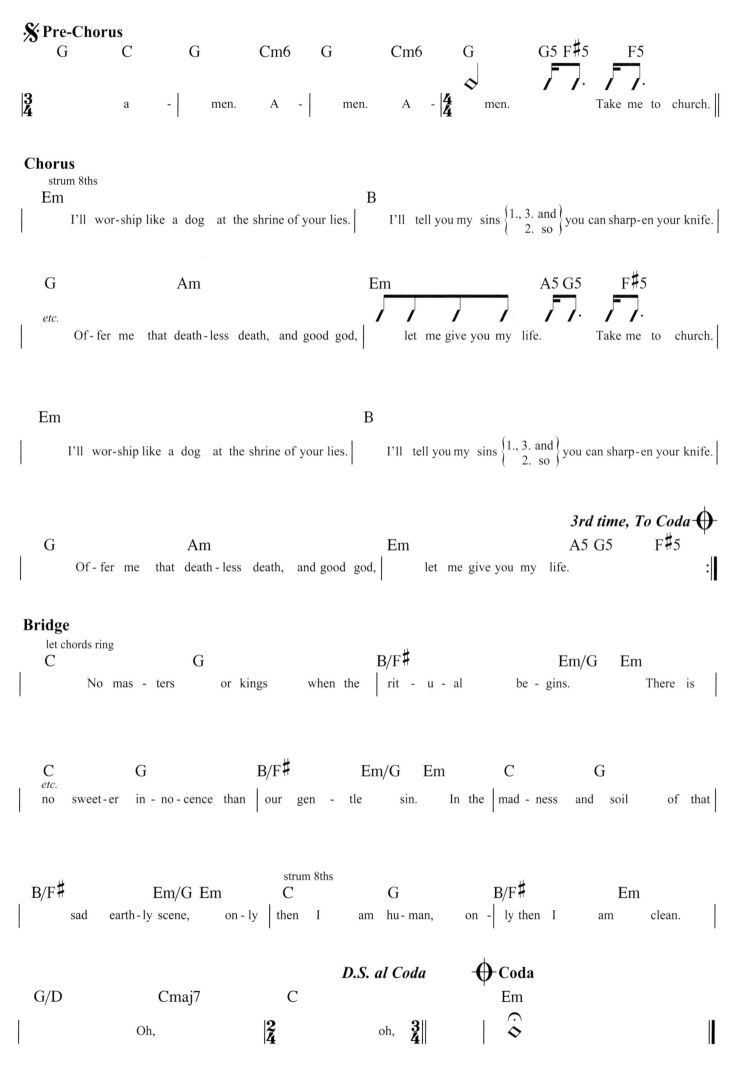

HAL LEONARD GUITAR CHEAT SHEETS

The Hal Leonard Cheat Sheets series includes lyrics, chord frames, and "rhythm tab" (cut-to-the-chase notation) to make playing easier than ever! No music reading is required, and all the songs are presented on two-page spreads to avoid page turns.

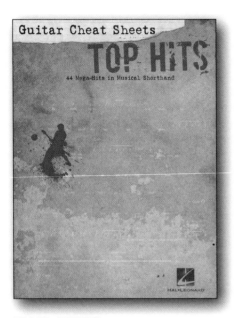

TOP HITS

44 pop favorites, including: Are You Gonna Be My Girl • Baby • Bad Day • Bubbly • Clocks • Crazy • Fireflies • Gives You Hell • Hey, Soul Sister • How to Save a Life • I Gotta Feeling Just the Way You Are • Lucky • Mercy • Mr. Brightside • Need You Now • Take Me Out • Toes • Use Somebody • Viva La Vida • You Belong with Me • and more.
00701646 ....$14.99

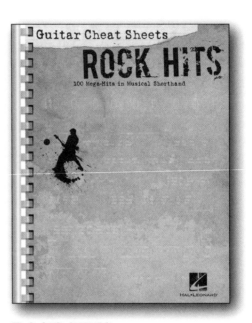

ROCK HITS

44 songs, including: Are You Gonna Go My Way • Black Hole Sun • Counting Blue Cars • Float On • Friday I'm in Love • Gives You Hell • Grenade • Jeremy • Kryptonite • Push • Scar Tissue • Semi-Charmed Life • Smells like Teen Spirit • Smooth • Thnks Fr Th Mmrs • Two Princes • Use Somebody • Viva La Vida • Where Is the Love • You Oughta Know • and more.
00702392 ....$24.99

ACOUSTIC HITS

100 unplugged megahits in musical shorthand: All Apologies • Crazy Little Thing Called Love • Creep • Daughter • Every Rose Has Its Thorn • Hallelujah • I'm Yours • The Lazy Song • Little Lion Man • Love Story • More Than Words • Patience • Strong Enough • 21 Guns • Wanted Dead or Alive • Wonderwall • and more.
00702391 ....$24.99

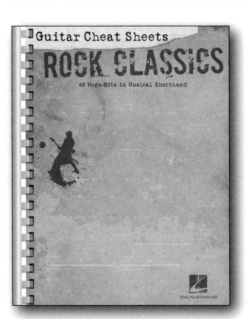

ROCK CLASSICS

Nearly 50 classics, including: All Right Now • Barracuda • Born to Be Wild • Carry on Wayward Son • Cat Scratch Fever • Free Ride • Layla • Message in a Bottle • Paranoid • Proud Mary • Rhiannon • Rock and Roll All Nite • Slow Ride • Smoke on the Water • Sweet Home Alabama • Welcome to the Jungle • You Shook Me All Night Long • and more.
00702393 ....$24.99

HAL•LEONARD®
CORPORATION
7777 W. BLUEMOUND RD. P.O.BOX 13819 MILWAUKEE, WI 53213

Visit Hal Leonard online at **www.halleonard.com**   *Prices, contents, and availability subject to change without notice.*   0712

easy GUITAR play along

The easy Guitar play along® Series features streamlined transcriptions of your favorite songs. Just follow the tab, listen to the CD to hear how the guitar should sound, and then play along using the backing tracks. The CD is playable on any CD player, and is also enhanced to include the Amazing Slowdowner technology so Mac and PC users can adjust the recording to any tempo without changing the pitch!

INCLUDES TAB

1. ROCK CLASSICS
Jailbreak • Living After Midnight • Mississippi Queen • Rocks Off • Runnin' Down a Dream • Smoke on the Water • Strutter • Up Around the Bend.
00702560 Book/CD Pack.......$14.99

2. ACOUSTIC TOP HITS
About a Girl • I'm Yours • The Lazy Song • The Scientist • 21 Guns • Upside Down • What I Got • Wonderwall.
00702569 Book/CD Pack.......$14.99

3. ROCK HITS
All the Small Things • Best of You • Brain Stew (The Godzilla Remix) • Californication • Island in the Sun • Plush • Smells like Teen Spirit • Use Somebody.
00702570 Book/CD Pack.......$14.99

4. ROCK 'N' ROLL
Blue Suede Shoes • I Get Around • I'm a Believer • Jailhouse Rock • Oh, Pretty Woman • Peggy Sue • Runaway • Wake up Little Susie.
00702572 Book/CD Pack.....$14.99

5. ULTIMATE ACOUSTIC
Against the Wind • Babe, I'm Gonna Leave You • Come Monday • Free Fallin' • Give a Little Bit • Have You Ever Seen the Rain? • New Kid in Town • We Can Work It Out.
00702573 Book/CD Pack........$14.99

6. CHRISTMAS SONGS
Have Yourself a Merry Little Christmas • A Holly Jolly Christmas • The Little Drummer Boy • Run Rudolph Run • Santa Claus Is Comin' to Town • Silver and Gold • Sleigh Ride • Winter Wonderland.
00101879 Book/CD Pack.........$14.99

7. BLUES SONGS FOR BEGINNERS
Come On (Part 1) • Double Trouble • Gangster of Love • I'm Ready • Let Me Love You Baby • Mary Had a Little Lamb • San-Ho-Zay • T-Bone Shuffle.
00103235 Book/CD Pack.....$14.99

8. ACOUSTIC SONGS FOR BEGINNERS
Barely Breathing • Drive • Everlong • Good Riddance (Time of Your Life) • Hallelujah • Hey There Delilah • Lake of Fire • Photograph.
00103240 Book/CD Pack.....$14.99

9. ROCK SONGS FOR BEGINNERS
Are You Gonna Be My Girl • Buddy Holly • Everybody Hurts • In Bloom • Otherside • The Rock Show • Santa Monica • When I Come Around.
00103255 Book/CD Pack.....$14.99

10. GREEN DAY
Basket Case • Boulevard of Broken Dreams • Good Riddance (Time of Your Life) • Holiday • Longview • 21 Guns • Wake Me up When September Ends • When I Come Around.
00122322 Book/CD Pack $14.99

11. NIRVANA
All Apologies • Come As You Are • Heart Shaped Box • Lake of Fire • Lithium • The Man Who Sold the World • Rape Me • Smells like Teen Spirit.
00122325 Book/CD Pack $14.99

12. TAYLOR SWIFT
Fifteen • Love Story • Mean • Picture to Burn • Red • We Are Never Ever Getting Back Together • White Horse • You Belong with Me.
00122326 Book/CD Pack $16.99

HAL•LEONARD® CORPORATION
7777 W. BLUEMOUND RD. P.O. BOX 13819 MILWAUKEE, WI 53213

www.halleonard.com

Prices, contents, and availability subject to change without notice.

0214